MOSES THE
USED BY

BOOK 3 (TOLD FROM EXODUS 4–13)

CARINE MACKENZIE
Illustrated by
Graham Kennedy

© Copyright Carine Mackenzie 2008
Published by Christian Focus Publications,
Geanies House, Fearn, Tain, Ross-shire, IV20 1TW, Scotland, U.K.
www.christianfocus.com
Printed in China

Moses went to Egypt and met with the leaders of the Hebrews. His brother Aaron told them how God had spoken to Moses, promising to free his people from slavery. Moses performed miracles in front of the people and they believed and worshipped God.

They then visited Pharaoh and asked him to let the people go into the desert to make sacrifice to God. Pharaoh was furious. "I will make their work even harder. They will have to gather the straw themselves and still make the same number of bricks."

Pharaoh would not let them go.
    God reminded Moses of his promise to free his people.

Pharaoh's heart was hard and cruel. He refused to listen to Moses and Aaron. God told Moses what to do.

When Pharaoh went out to the river in the morning, Aaron stretched out his staff over the water. The water of the river immediately turned to blood.

The fish died. There was no fresh water to drink for seven whole days. But still Pharaoh was stubborn.

The Lord sent more and more plagues each time Pharaoh refused to let the people go.

Swarms of frogs covered the land – into houses – in the beds – even in the ovens and cooking bowls.

Then gnats covered the people and the animals. Swarms of flies tormented the Egyptians but not the Hebrew people.

The fifth plague that God sent to the Egyptians affected all their animals. All the horses, donkeys, camels, cows and sheep died. But the animals belonging to the Hebrews were spared.

Still Pharaoh did not get the message. Painful boils broke out on the Egyptians.

Then heavy hailstones flattened the crops. Pharaoh at last showed some remorse but as soon as the hail stopped, he became hard-hearted again.

Locusts plagued the land, eating any plant or leaf that was left after the hailstorms.

Then intense darkness covered the land for three days. The Egyptians could not see each other, or even move from their homes.

God kept his own people, the Hebrews, free from all these plagues.

"I will send one more plague on Pharaoh and the Egyptians," God told Moses, "and then he will let you go."

Moses went to warn Pharaoh. "At midnight every firstborn child in every family will die."

This was the most terrible punishment of all. Still Pharaoh would not listen.

God promised to keep his people safe.

Moses passed on God's instructions to each family. The best lamb of the flock was killed. The blood was then painted on the doorposts and lintel of the house.

When the angel of death passed through Egypt, he would pass over the houses marked with blood.

The families ate a special meal that night of roast lamb, unleavened bread and bitter herbs. Every year from then on, the Hebrew people held a special feast called The Passover Feast.

They remembered what God had done for them.

We must also remember what God has done for us in sending his Son, Jesus, to save his people from their sin.

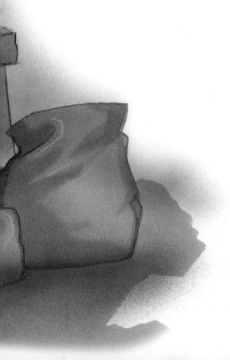

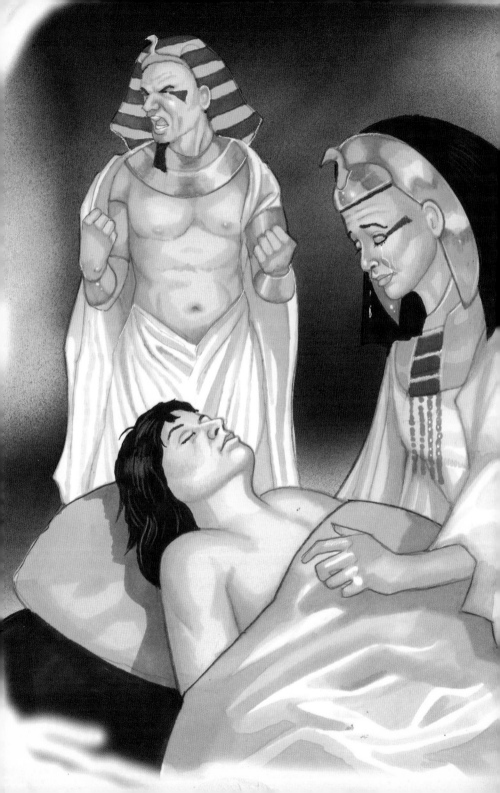

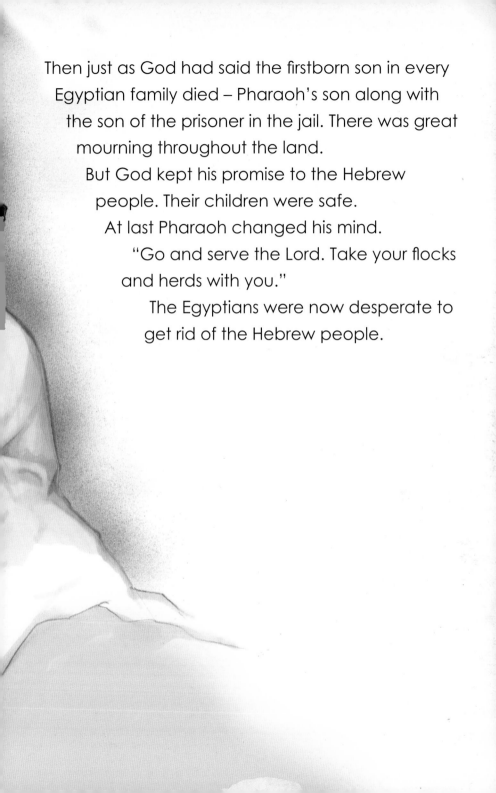

Then just as God had said the firstborn son in every Egyptian family died – Pharaoh's son along with the son of the prisoner in the jail. There was great mourning throughout the land.

But God kept his promise to the Hebrew people. Their children were safe.

At last Pharaoh changed his mind.

"Go and serve the Lord. Take your flocks and herds with you."

The Egyptians were now desperate to get rid of the Hebrew people.

At last God's promise came to pass. The people of God were set free from slavery in Egypt and started on their journey to the land of Canaan.

God guided them with a pillar of cloud during the day and a pillar of fire at night-time.

Once the Hebrew slaves were gone, Pharaoh had second thoughts. Who would do all the hard work now?

Pharaoh sent soldiers after them to bring them back but God was looking after them and he miraculously helped them to escape.

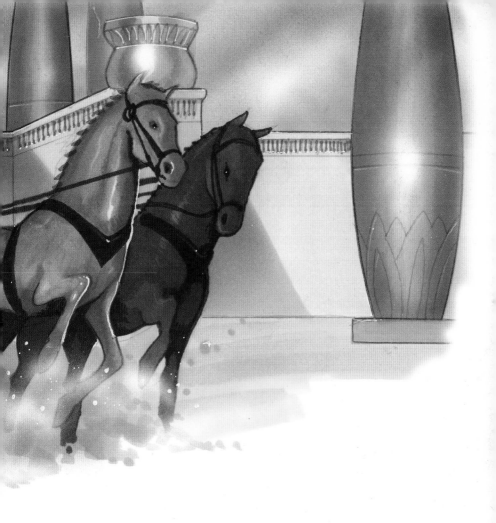

God used his servant Moses to carry out his plan to save his people from cruel slavery in Egypt. Although Moses did not feel fit for the task, God helped him.

Remember that God is always able to help you too.

Many more adventures follow as Moses and the Hebrew people travel on.

God has a wonderful plan to save his people from slavery to sin. His Son, the Lord Jesus Christ came to this world to die for the sins of his people.